Creative
Spinning

Alison Daykin and Jane Deane

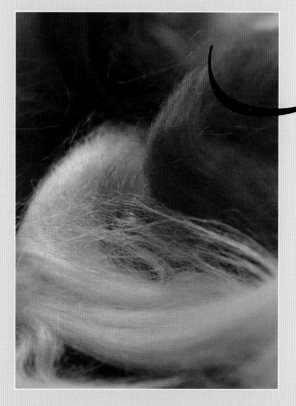

LARK BOOKS

A Division of Sterling Publishing Co., Inc.
New York / London

Library of Congress Cataloging-in-Publication Data
Daykin, Alison, 1954-
    Creative spinning / Alison Daykin and Jane Deane. -- 1st ed.
       p. cm.
    Includes index.
    ISBN-13: 978-1-60059-223-2 (pb-with flaps : alk. paper)
    ISBN-10: 1-60059-223-6 (pb-with flaps : alk. paper)
    1. Hand spinning. 2. Spun yarns. I. Deane, Jane, 1948- II. Title.
    TT847.D39 2008
    746.1'2--dc22
                                              2007022990

10 9 8 7 6 5 4 3 2 1

First Edition

Published by Lark Books, A Division of
Sterling Publishing Co., Inc.
387 Park Avenue South, New York, N.Y. 10016

First published 2007
Under the title CREATIVE SPINNING
By Gaia (an imprint, part of) Octopus Publishing Group Ltd
2–4 Heron Quays, Docklands, London E14 4JP

© 2007 Octopus Publishing Group Ltd
All rights reserved
Americanization © 2007 Octopus Publishing Group Ltd

Distributed in Canada by Sterling Publishing,
c/o Canadian Manda Group, 165 Dufferin Street
Toronto, Ontario, Canada M6K 3H6

If you have questions or comments about this book, please contact:
Lark Books
67 Broadway
Asheville, NC 28801
(828) 253-0467

Manufactured in China

ISBN 13: 978-1-60059-223-2
ISBN 10: 1-60059-223-6

For information about custom editions, special sales, premium and corporate purchases, please contact Sterling Special Sales Department at 800-805-5489 or specialsales@sterlingpub.com.

contents

Introduction

Spinning is a skill that has been practiced by humankind for thousands of years. The earliest societies spun whatever fiber nature provided for them – the fibers of animals such as sheep, alpaca, camel and goat in cold areas; and the fibers of plants in warmer regions, such as cotton, linen, ramie (nettle fiber) and hemp. Silk is a unique fiber in that it is the spun thread of the caterpillars of various silk moth species, and for hundreds of years the Chinese and Japanese closely guarded the secret of its production.

Why spin when the shops today are bursting with wonderful yarns, beautiful garments and domestic textiles? Well, spinning is a very relaxing activity and in today's world of hustle and bustle such activities are essential for our physical and mental wellbeing. It is a craft that keeps us in touch with our earliest human roots. Many spinners go on to learn to dye and weave their yarns. Some spinners grow their own dye plants and produce their own fibers for spinning, either by keeping animals or growing flax, nettles and other fibrous plants.

The modern spinner has many advantages over his or her ancient counterpart. Thanks to the ease of modern communications we are able to source fibers from all over the world and can try spinning anything from Angora to yak. Today hand spinners also have the opportunity to spin hi-tech fibers from such sources as recycled plastic bottles. We are also fortunate to be able to choose from a wider range of equipment, going from the really basic biodegradable spindle made from an apple and a twig up to wheels that incorporate all that technology can provide. However, a thread spun on a hand spindle can equal

Above: Traditional flyer wheel.

or excel that spun on the most sophisticated spinning equipment. More importantly, perhaps, by spinning your own yarn you have the opportunity to create something that is uniquely yours, either to keep or to give as a very special gift.

Above: Top whorl spindle.

Equipment

You need very little equipment for basic spinning. A hand spindle is enough to start with. However, a spinning wheel makes spinning easier and more efficient, and there are several different types of wheel available to choose from.

For preparing wool fibers for long draw spinning you will need proper carders. These resemble a pair of large wooden hairbrushes and are covered with a carding cloth from which bent wire teeth protrude. An ordinary dog comb, preferably with wide teeth, will do for combing fibers in preparation for spinning using the worsted method.

Your spinning wheel comes provided with bobbins and a Lazy Kate, a stand for storing the bobbins and also an aid to plying. Another useful piece of equipment, for winding skeins, is a niddy noddy.

You will need two bowls or buckets and shampoo or detergent for washing fleeces and for finishing yarn. Dishwashing liquid and shampoo are ideal.

How to use this book

The aim of this book is to help you start spinning, and to encourage you to experiment creatively with the wealth of wonderful fibers available.

The first part of the book explains all the general techniques that you will need, and shows you how to put them into practice through step-by-step illustrations. It offers an overview of the fibers you are likely to work with, before moving on to the preparatory techniques of carding and combing fibers.

After learning how to prepare fibers there are instructions to get you actually spinning, using a simple spindle and wool fleece. The instructions then move on to describe the various types of spinning wheel and show you how to use a wheel.

Once you are familiar with spinning 'singles yarn', the first yarn produced from fibers, you can progress to two-plying and three-plying yarns.

Further techniques follow to enable you to construct and spin a variety of fancy yarns, including several silk spinning methods.

All this practical information will give you the confidence to spin creatively, and the bulk of the book presents 30 projects for you to try. They are arranged by fiber, and we have used a wide range of color that will delight the eye and inspire you.

Each project provides information on what materials you will need to spin a 4 oz (100 g) hank of yarn and instructions on how to spin it, referring you back to the earlier 'How to spin' section when necessary. All the projects can be spun using either the basic drop spindle technique (see pages 13–14) or the basic spinning wheel technique (see pages 16–17) unless otherwise specified. The projects include beautiful photographs of the unspun fibers, the spun yarn and a swatch of the yarn knitted in the stockinette stitch.

Please note, too, that all the instructions are written for a right-handed spinner. If you are spinning left handed, all you need to do is reverse the instructions and follow the illustrations by placing the book in front of a mirror.

How to spin

Several stages are needed for successful spinning. First you need to prepare the fibers by carding or combing, depending on the spinning technique you will be using. Then there is the spinning process, using a spindle or wheel, producing 'singles' yarns that can then be plied to produce yarns that are suitable for knitting or weaving. Finally, the yarns must go through 'finishing' by washing and 'setting' to ensure consistency.

Working with fibers

Spinners work with a variety of fibers such as wool, animal hair, silk and vegetable fibers.

WOOL

Wool is the shorn, natural coat of sheep and is the ideal fiber to learn to spin with. The length or staple of the fibers varies between 2–16 in (5–40 cm), depending on the breed.

Wool is warm, light and elastic, and also has the ability to absorb water. It is important to consider the suitability of the fleece you select for a project. For example, you would not make a baby's shawl from a tough hill and mountain breed wool, nor would you use a soft shortwool and down fleece to make a floor rug.

Wool is available to hand spinners as raw, unwashed fleece from farmers or specialist hand spinning suppliers. 'Tops' (or 'slivers') are wool fibers that have been commercially washed and combed, and are ready for use.

Unwashed fleece can be dirty. This dirt can build up in carders and combs, or the orifice and hooks of your wheel, and may transfer itself to other fibers you spin. So, it is a good idea to wash a fleece before use.

Do not try to wash a whole fleece at one time unless you have a very large container and plenty of drying space. Wool's capacity to absorb water is astounding and a fleece can swell alarmingly when plunged into water.

ANIMAL HAIR

Animal hair that can be spun includes camel, alpaca, cashmere, mohair from the Angora goat and fibers from the Angora rabbit. These fibers can be obtained direct from the breeder or as ready-prepared tops.

Small amounts of animal hair blended with wool give attractive and unusual yarns. Blending reduces the

Staple length

Knowing the 'staple' – that is, the length – of the fibers helps you determine which method of preparation and which spinning technique to use. Short fibers are suited to carding and long draw spinning, while long fibers can be prepared by combing and are spun with the worsted technique.

slipperiness of the fibers, making them easier to handle and produces a lighter, airier yarn. Animal fibers are finer than wool and require more twist when spinning.

Animal fibers have less grease than wool, but if they seem very dirty a gentle soak in warm water and mild detergent, followed by a rinse, is all that is required. Staple length varies considerably between different breeds.

SILK

Silk fibers are available as tops from specialist spinning suppliers. Silk is extremely light, warm in cold weather and cool in the heat. Its surface has an attractive luster. Silk is a strong fiber, but is weakened when damp.

COTTON

Cotton fibers come in several qualities and, in general, the longer the fibers the finer they are. The short fibers, known as noils, are the coarsest, with a staple length of about ¾ in (2 cm). The longer, finer fibers have a staple length of between 1–2 in (2.5–5 cm). All fibers are available from specialist hand spinning suppliers and longer fibers come in the form of combed tops.

RAMIE

Ramie has a luster and fineness that rivals silk. It is extremely strong and is inelastic, so it is sometimes used as a replacement for linen. Ramie blends well with other fibers. It is obtained from specialist hand spinning suppliers in the form of tops, with a staple length between 4–10 in (10–25 cm), and also in noils form.

BAMBOO

Bamboo fibers have unique anti-bacterial properties and are 100 percent biodegradable. Bamboo is noted for its breathability and coolness. Bamboo fibers are available from specialist hand spinning suppliers as loose fibers and tops.

SOYA

Soya fibers are soft and lustrous, resembling tussah silk, and are likened to cashmere. Fabrics made from soya fiber drape well, have good laundering qualities, are durable and wear well. The fibers are obtained from specialist hand spinning suppliers in tops form and have a staple length of 2 in (5 cm).

FLAX

Flax fibers are processed to produce linen yarn. Linen garments are absorbent and allow the skin to breathe. They wear well, soften with repeated laundering and maintain their shape.

The best quality fibers, known as linen flax, can be obtained in the form of 'stricks', which are long, thick locks of fibers. Shorter fibers, known as 'tow' flax, are available as combed tops. The short or broken fibers that remain after flax has been processed are called linen noils. You can purchase all these flax fibers from specialist suppliers.

Washing a fleece

To wash a fleece, lay it out on newspaper or plastic sheeting, preferably outside. Look closely and remove any foul material. Sort the fleece into qualities –you will see where the animal has rubbed against fences and the fleece is worn. When your first batch of fleece is ready to wash, give it a good shake so that any loose debris drops out.

Lower the fleece into a bowl of very hot water and detergent. Press down gently until the fleece is submerged, avoiding any agitation, which will cause the wool to 'felt'.

Leave the fleece to soak until the water is just cool enough for your hands to bear, then lift it out and put it into a bowl of rinsing water that is the same temperature as the water you have just removed the fleece from.

Repeat the rinsing process until the wool is clean. Gently tease out the fibers and place the wool in a pillowcase or mesh laundry bag. Spin dry on a gentle setting to remove excess water.

Fiber preparation

You can spin fibers without any preparation, but if you wish to have a greater degree of control in spinning then you will need to know how to card and comb fibers.

Carding gives light, airy yarns that are suitable for knitwear and for items that will not be subjected to hard use. Once the fibers are carded they are spun using the long draw technique (see page 18).

Combing prepares the fibers for tightly spun yarns that will resist abrasion and pilling. Combed fibers are spun using the worsted spinning technique (see page 19). The examples of carding and combing shown here use wool fleece.

CARDING

Carding produces a haphazard arrangement of fibers that will trap the air as the material is spun. Fibers that are to be carded should not have a staple length that is longer than the depth of the carding cloth.

Carders for hand spinners consist of two flat or curved pieces of wood, approximately 8 x 4 in (20 x 10 cm), each with a handle. The face of each carder is covered with a 'cloth', usually made of leather or rubber. The surface of the cloth is pierced by short wires, bent at a slight angle, and it is these wires that 'brush' the fibers.

1 Tease the wool to open up the fibers. Then place small quantities of fleece on one of a pair of carders.

2 Using the other carder, gently pull the fibers across the surface of the first carder and straighten the fibers. This action is termed a 'pass'. Try not to let the fibers become embedded in the teeth of the carders – the action should be light. After one or two passes you will be ready to transfer the fibers to the other carder.

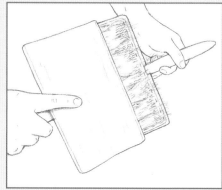

3 Hold the 'empty' carder with the edge nearest the handle against the lower edge of the 'full' carder. Catch the fibers with the teeth of the empty carder and lift it up towards the handle edge of the full carder. As you do this, the fibers will transfer from one carder to the other. Change hands so that the full carder is in your left hand and repeat the carding process. Continue until the fibers lie straight with no obvious lumps or bumps.

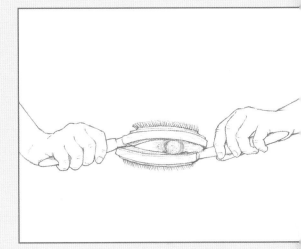

4 When you are satisfied that your fibers have been sufficiently carded, strip the fibers from the full carder as in Step 3 and then transfer them gently back onto the empty carder so that they are lying gently on the top of the teeth and are not caught in the carder. Take the empty carder in your right hand, wood side facing the fibers and at an angle of 90 degrees, and just catch the end of the fibers with the bottom edge of the empty carder. Fold these end fibers back onto the carder and press *gently*, catching the fibers lightly onto the carding cloth to secure them.

5 Push the right-hand carder up the carding cloth, rolling the fibers up as you go. The fibers will start to form a light roll – a rolag.

6 Lift the rolag from the carder and place it on the back of the carder. With the carders back-to-back and with the rolag between them, gently roll it between them.

Right: The finished rolag should look like this.

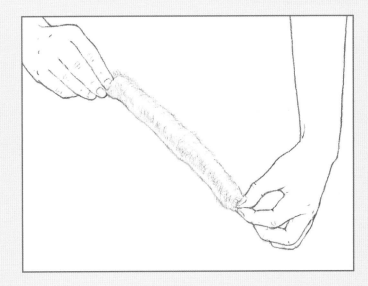

COMBING

The object of combing is to produce an orderly arrangement of parallel fibers from which the short fibers, known as 'noil', have been removed. This gives a dense, tightly spun yarn that is resistant to pilling.

For most hand-spinning purposes, and certainly for beginners, an ordinary dog comb is quite adequate to use. For 'true' wool combing, experienced spinners will always comb the fleece in one direction, from the butt (sheared end) down to the tip (outside end), but this is not practical using a dog comb. Traditional combs are expensive, and are heavy pieces of equipment, so think carefully before investing in a set.

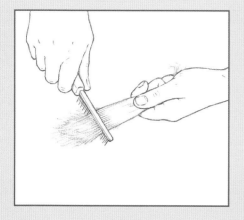 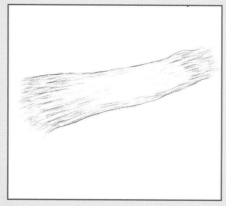 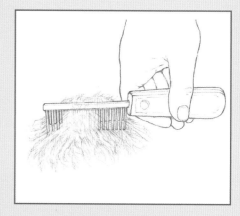

1 Take a lock of fleece in one hand, holding it firmly halfway along, near the butt end. Place the comb in the fibers near the tips and pull the comb through, working backwards through the lock towards your hand. Repeat until you are satisfied that the fleece is free from tangles, that the fibers are lying parallel, and that the short fibers are collecting in the comb and being stripped out of the lock. Then turn the lock around and repeat the process with the uncombed end.

2 The resulting lock will look smooth and even, and the individual fibers will be separated.

3 The short fibers will be left in the comb. These can be put to one side to be carded and spun using the long draw technique.

Spindle spinning

Spinning is a very simple technique. If you take a lock of fleece and twist the lock several times it will form into a cohesive unit by the action of twisting and you will have made a very simple yarn.

Obviously, it would take forever to produce a yarn by simple twisting by hand, and the results might well not justify the effort. Using a spindle to put a twist in the yarn makes the job much quicker and allows you to 'draft' the fiber – that is, to pull out the individual fibers from the mass so that you can handle them more easily. The result is a more attractive and useful yarn.

Hand spindles

A spindle is, at its simplest, a stick with a weight attached. In this book a drop spindle is used to illustrate basic steps in spinning. The stick, or shaft, goes through a wooden disc, known as the weight or whorl, towards the lower end of the stick. The top end of the stick, about 1 in (2–3 cm) down, has a notch cut into it. There are several variations on the design of a spindle: some have the whorl at the top and a hook to guide the yarn rather than a notch; some are meant to spin freely, others to be supported in a bowl. They all work on exactly the same principle.

USING A DROP SPINDLE

To begin spinning, you need a spindle, some fibers to spin and a piece of spun yarn – commercial yarn is suitable to use. The piece of spun yarn is called the 'leader' and is used to attach the fibers to start the spinning off.

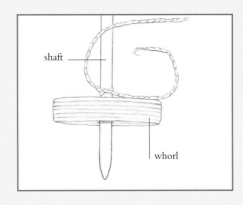

1 Take the spun yarn, or leader, and tie one end onto the spindle shaft just above the whorl.

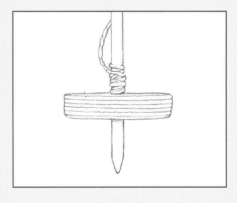

2 Wrap the yarn a few times round the shaft to give some grip.

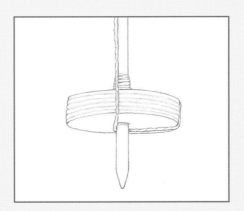

3 Take the yarn down, round the lower end of the shaft, under the whorl, and back up to the top of the spindle.

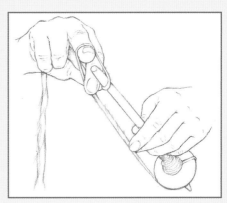

4 Secure the leader at the top of the shaft with a half-hitch knot in the notch.

14

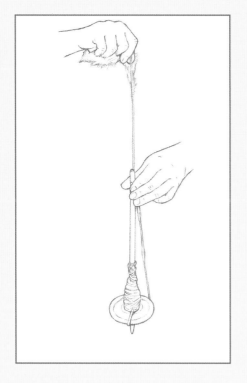

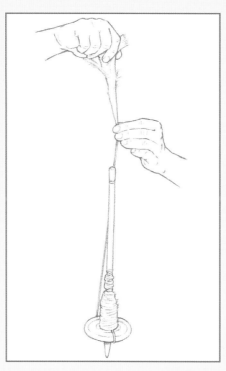

Tip Try the individual steps one at a time, laying the spindle on a flat surface. It is invaluable to try to understand the sequence while not also having to control twist, spindle and fibers at the same time.

5 To join the fiber to the leader, take the prepared fibers in your right hand, the spindle in your left (reverse, if left handed; it may be more comfortable). Twist the spindle clockwise, let go of the spindle, but keep holding onto the leader yarn so that the spindle is spinning freely. Pull a few fibers from the mass with your left hand, still with a firm grip on the leader, and offer them to the leader yarn a little way down from the top. You should be able to see the fibers twisting with the leader yarn and joining onto it.

6 As the twist runs up the leader and into the drawn-out fibers, forming the yarn, hold the newly spun yarn gently in your left hand, pinching the yarn between your finger and thumb to prevent the twist running into the fiber mass. Release a new bundle of fibers to spin by pulling your right hand up, away from the spindle, allowing a few fibers to remain between your left and right hands while continuing to keep a firm hold on the fiber mass. Release your left finger and thumb so that the twist can enter the fibers you have drawn between your hands. Repeat this sequence of drawing the fibers from

the mass and allowing the twist to enter them until your yarn is too long to spin comfortably and your spindle is nearing the floor!

Stop spinning, undo the half-hitch from the notch, release the yarn from below the whorl and wind the handspun yarn around the bottom of the shaft, above the whorl. Leave enough unwound yarn to go back under the whorl and up to the notch, ready for you to start spinning again.

Continue spinning until you have spun the amount of yarn you wish, or until the spindle is full. Once the spindle is nearing its limit it will become difficult to maintain the spin. Stop spinning and unwind the yarn from the spindle onto a cardboard roll, or a bobbin, or into a ball. When you reach the leader you will be able to pull your spun yarn free from the leader, leaving the leader on the spindle for when you begin again.

Wheel spinning

A spinning wheel is basically a horizontal spindle held in place by supports and driven by a wheel. The first spinning wheels were exactly this; the wheel spun by hand and the spindle was connected to the wheel by a band that ran round the spindle whorl and the wheel, so that when the wheel rotated the spindle did as well.

With the early wheels the twist entered the fibers as the spinner held them so that the newly spun yarn bounced from the tip of the spindle, sending the spin up to the drafting area. To wind yarn onto the spindle required a separate action: the spinner had to stop the wheel putting twist into the yarn and allow it to wind onto the spindle. These wheels are known as great wheels or walking wheels, because to spin a length of yarn the spinner walked backwards as far as possible before the yarn needed to be wound onto the spindle.

Flyer and bobbin wheels

The invention of the flyer was a huge technological leap forward. The flyer enables the yarn to be wound onto the bobbin at the same time as the twist is put into the yarn. The wheel is much smaller and is driven by a foot treadle, allowing the spinner to sit at the wheel and spin, using both hands to control the yarn formation.

The flyer wheel comes in various shapes and sizes. All the wheels work according to the same principles, although there are two different systems for controlling the relative speeds of the flyer and bobbin – many modern wheels have both of these systems.

Double drive wheels

A wheel with a double drive band has a long drive band that goes around the wheel and flyer *and* around the wheel and bobbin whorl. One long band controls both units. If you have a double drive wheel, you adjust the tension by turning a screw or knob that alters the relative positions of the wheel, flyer and bobbin. On most double drive wheels you increase the distance between the drive wheel and the flyer to increase the tension.

Scotch tension wheels

A Scotch tension wheel uses one band that goes around the wheel and flyer, and a separate arrangement that controls the speed of the bobbin. This is commonly a band, attached at one end to a knob that can be tightened and loosened as necessary; that goes over the bobbin whorl and is attached at the other end to a spring or an elastic band secured by a hook to the flyer unit. If you have a Scotch tension wheel, you adjust the wheel/flyer relationship and the flyer/bobbin relationship separately. It may be sufficient simply to tighten the band that controls the speed of the bobbin whorl.

Wheel tension

You need to adjust the tension on your wheel as the bobbin fills – new yarn travels a very short distance around the shaft of an empty bobbin, but much further around a full bobbin. If you treadle and draw out the fibers at the same rate throughout the spinning without compensating for the increased distance the yarn has to travel as the bobbin fills, you may find you have a highly twisted yarn at the shaft end of the bobbin and a lightly twisted yarn at the outside. To maintain consistency of twist, adjust the tension on the wheel.

USING A SPINNING WHEEL

It is a good idea to practice treadling the wheel while there is no yarn being spun, perhaps while you are watching television or reading a book. Try to keep the wheel turning consistently in one direction – it will want to reverse the turn if it can – and at the same time try to treadle as slowly as you can while maintaining momentum. If you can control the wheel comfortably with your foot, it is one less thing to cope with when you have fibers to deal with!

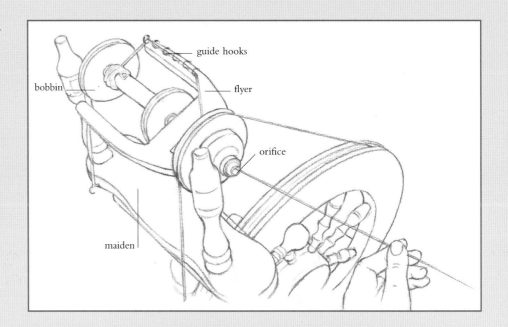

1 Just as with the spindle, wheel spinning requires a leader yarn to be attached to the bobbin. To begin, the leader goes around the bobbin, into one of the guide hooks that are screwed into the flyer and comes through the orifice at the front of the flyer unit. If you put the yarn through the hook furthest from you, and carry it through the rest of the hooks to the orifice, you will be able to see the yarn forming as you spin.

2 Begin to treadle the wheel as slowly as you can manage – this will stop the leader yarn from being drawn too rapidly onto the bobbin and give you a chance to attach the fibers. Pull a few fibers from the mass as for spindle spinning (see pages 13–14) and allow these fibers to attach themselves to the leader.

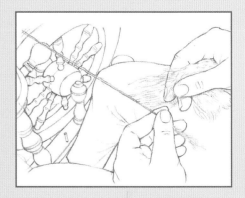

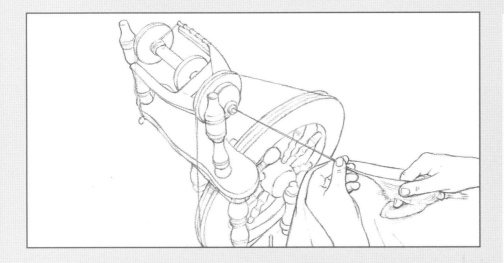

3 Once the fibers are attached, let the twist run up the drafted fibers and wind onto the bobbin, as you continue to draft.

4 When spinning a singles yarn, decide whether you want to use it as a singles (that is, unplied) or if you are going to ply it. Plying requires respinning the yarns together, turning the wheel in the opposite direction to that of the initial spinning and potentially taking out some of the twist. In order not to take out all the twist that holds the fibers together you will need to ensure that there is enough twist in the singles yarn. A good guide is to put enough twist in the spun yarn so that it is straight when held under gentle tension, but twists back on itself when the tension is released.

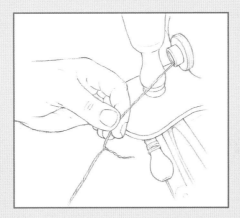

Once the spinning is complete, release the tension from the wheel, so that the bobbin runs freely, take the yarn back through the orifice and wind the yarn off into a skein or ball.

Tip New spinners usually hold onto the newly formed yarn, allowing so much twist into the fibers that the yarn corkscrews and breaks as it draws onto the bobbin. There is a tendency to overcorrect this by not allowing enough twist into the fibers, causing the yarn to disintegrate before it reaches the bobbin. This is all quite normal! Do not despair: just keep practicing. Before long you will be spinning a yarn that will please you.

Long draw spinning

This method of spinning, also known as woollen or long woollen draw spinning, is used for producing light, lofty yarns that are suitable for knitwear. The preparation of rolags (see page 11) is vital for this technique. The instructions below show the technique using a spinning wheel but you can also use a spindle for long draw spinning.

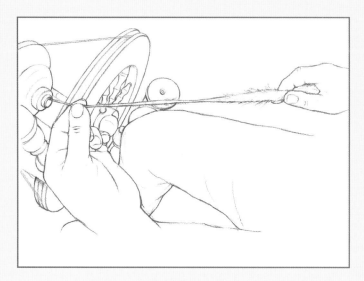

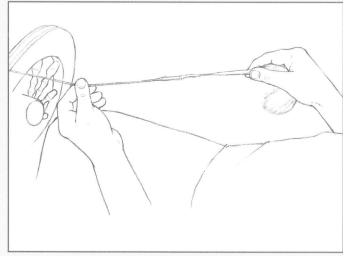

1 Attach the rolag to the leader (see page 16). Hold the yarn near the orifice, with your left hand. Hold the rolag lightly in your right hand. Gently pinch the yarn passing between your left finger and thumb. Release about ½ in (12 mm) of the rolag, holding the rest firmly, and begin to pull the rolag away from the wheel, while at the same time allowing a little twist through the finger and thumb of the left hand into the drafted fibers.

2 As you continue to pull back on the forming yarn and gradually release a little twist into the fibers, the yarn will begin to feel elastic, rather like chewing gum. Continue until you have stretched your arm as far as you can. If you feel the yarn needs a little more twist continue to treadle the wheel once or twice while holding the yarn still, then allow it to wind quickly onto the bobbin and begin to draw out the next section of the rolag.

Worsted spinning

The worsted technique keeps the fibers parallel to enable the spinner to produce dense, tightly spun yarn. The fibers are combed thoroughly first, either by hand or commercially, as in the case of 'tops'. The instructions below show the technique using a spinning wheel but you can also use a spindle for worsted spinning.

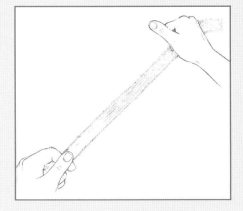

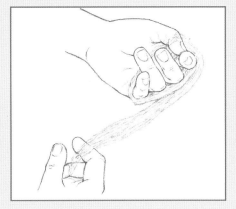

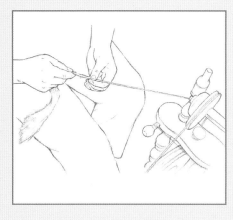

1 Using your combed fibers, draw out the fibers by hand until you have the amount of fibers required for the thickness of your singles yarn. Continue drafting in this way until all the fibers have been prepared. This long fine ribbon of fibers is known as a roving.

2 The rovings can be stored by inserting a little twist by hand and winding round your hand to form them into a little 'bird's nest'.

3 When ready to spin, attach these fibers to the leader and allow the twist to run up into the fibers without further drafting.

Woollen or worsted?

A significant difference between woollen and worsted spinning is that in woollen spinning the twist enters the fiber supply while drafting is taking place; in worsted spinning the twist does not enter the supply until drafting is complete.

Plying

Singles yarns often have too much twist and most projects require a 'balanced' yarn. Plying two or more singles yarns together helps to balance the yarn as it removes the excess twist as well as providing extra strength.

When you spin on a wheel or spindle the yarn has a twist in it. If you turn the wheel in a clockwise direction you will get a Z spin (so called because the angle of twist in the yarn looks like the letter Z). If you spin the spindle or wheel counterclockwise, the spin will be S (because the angle of twist resembles a letter S).

Z and S twist become important when you want to ply two single yarns together or if you want to create a fancy yarn.

Tip It is a good idea to check for balance throughout your plying.

TWO-PLY YARN

To make a two-ply knitting yarn, first spin two bobbins of Z (clockwise) singles yarn. Place these bobbins in a Lazy Kate and put a new bobbin onto the wheel. To ply the two singles yarns together you will need to spin them together from the Lazy Kate onto the new bobbin, using a leader.

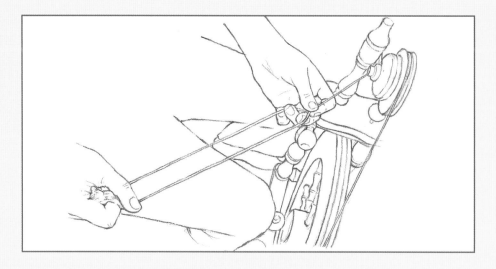

1 Keeping the two Z singles parallel, turn the spinning wheel in the counterclockwise S direction.

2 Allow the twist to move down the two singles, causing them to twist around each other. Allow the newly plied yarn to run onto the spinning wheel bobbin.

REPAIRING A BREAK

Occasionally one of the singles can break during plying. Overlap the broken ends and allow the twist to move down both singles, securing the overlapped ends of the broken thread in the ply.

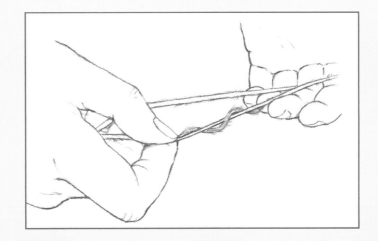

BALANCING THE PLY

For most purposes you will want to produce a balanced yarn – that is, one that does not contain extra twist that might cause distortions when knitted or woven. To check that your plying is producing a balanced yarn, ply 12–18 in (30–45 cm) of yarn, but do not let it run onto the bobbin. Allow this length of yarn to loop in front of the orifice. You can then check if it is overplied or underplied – in both cases the plied yarn itself will twist. A balanced plied yarn has no extra twist and falls in a loop.

Overplied yarn

If the plied yarn naturally twists to the left of the thread from the orifice (clockwise) it is overplied. To remove some of the twist, move your hand back to let the extra twist run into the unplied yarn.

Underplied

If the yarn naturally twists to the right of the thread from the orifice (counterclockwise), it is underplied. To correct add more twist by treadling one or two times more.

Balanced yarn

The plied yarn is balanced if it hangs in an untwisted loop.

Tip If you have bobbins on your Lazy Kate that are filled with yarn from which you are not plying, make sure that the ends of the unwanted yarns are securely fastened. These can develop a life of their own and tangle themselves in with the active yarns you are plying if they get a chance! If you do not have a Lazy Kate you can improvise one using knitting needles pushed through a shoebox.

THREE-PLY YARN

It is occasionally useful to make a three-ply yarn from a single bobbin. The process is similar to making a crochet chain. This is a particularly useful technique when you have a multicolored singles yarn and want to ply it without getting the muddy effect that can happen when you ply two singles yarns together. Also called Navajo plying, this method produces a firm yarn that is suitable for many different purposes.

To make a three-ply yarn take an empty bobbin with leader attached and put it on the wheel. Place the full bobbin on a Lazy Kate a little further away from the wheel than you would for normal two-plying.

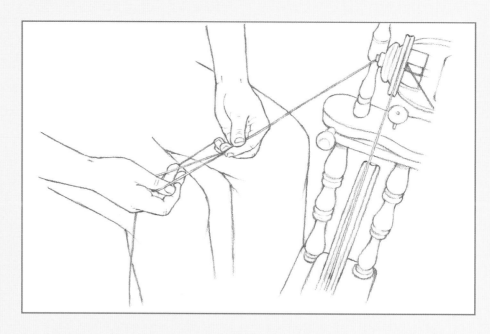

1 Attach the yarn to the leader and make a loop in the yarn, with the loop on top of the yarn.

 Tip If you are buying a second-hand wheel try to ensure that it has three bobbins. If it is a modern wheel you are likely to be able to obtain spares easily. If it is a very old wheel you may have to wind your spun yarn onto cardboard tubes from which you can ply.

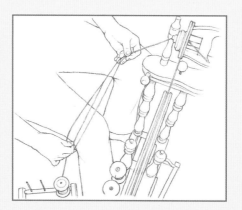

2 Turn the wheel in the S direction (counterclockwise), enlarging the loop, and pull the lower thread through the loop.

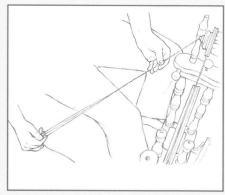

3 Allow the three threads to twist together as you continue to pull the lower thread up to form another loop and so on.

Yarn finishing

Spun yarn needs several 'finishing' processes before it is ready to be used for knitting or weaving. However skilled the spinner, there will be small variables in the yarn and finishing the yarn can make a dramatic difference to the success of the end product.

Washing removes any final traces of dirt, but also enables the yarn to be 'set'. Setting the yarn ensures that it will behave consistently in use; it evens out irregularities in a skein and, perhaps more importantly, all the skeins that will be used in a single garment. It is always wise to finish the yarns for a single garment together, so that they receive identical treatment.

MAKING A SKEIN

When the bobbin is full after plying, remove the spun plied yarn and make it into a skein. This will make the yarn easier to handle and use. The most efficient way to make a skein of yarn is to use a niddy noddy.

Grasp the end of the yarn in the left hand and hold onto the central post of the niddy noddy. Following the line of the yarn in the illustration, wind all the yarn from the bobbin onto the niddy noddy. The niddy noddy stays in one hand, but will 'nid-nod' as you move it to facilitate the winding.

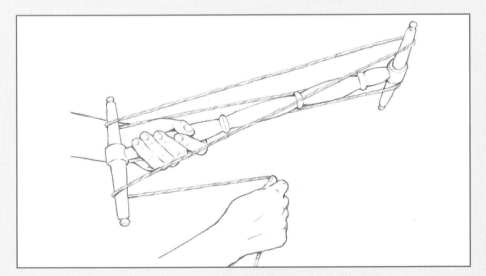

WASHING AND SETTING

Wash the skein as you would a fleece, but in slightly cooler water. Place in a pillowcase or laundry bag and spin it dry or roll it in a towel to remove the excess water.

To set the yarn, double the skein over the bottom bar of a plastic triangular coat hanger and put the hook of a second hanger through the loops at the bottom. The weight of the second hanger is just enough to tension the yarn without stretching it as it dries. When the yarn is completely dry, it will be ready for use.

TWISTING A SKEIN

Skeins are easier to store if they are twisted into a more compact shape.

Once completely dry, grasp the ends of the skein and twist several times. Bring the two ends of the skein together, allowing them to twist round each other and insert one end into the other.

Fancy yarn techniques

You can produce a multitude of lovely 'fancy' yarns by introducing 'irregularities' in your spinning. Many of the techniques used for creating these variations have different names in different countries and even in different regions of the same country, and as many as possible are given here. There are three opportunities to introduce irregularities when constructing and designing hand spun fancy yarns: in the preparation process, in the spinning process and/or in the plying process.

You can produce other attractive yarns using silk (see pages 28–29).

SLUB YARN

Slubs are formed by allowing thicker areas of undrafted fibers to move into the twist during the spinning process. These thicker areas can be made at regular intervals, irregular intervals, in both singles or just one.

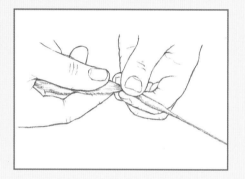

1 Using combed fibers, at the point where the twist meets the drafted fibers, pinch a lump of drafted fibers between your thumb and forefinger.

2 Pull the hands apart until a thinner area of drafted fibers appears and allow the twist to jump over the thicker area into this thin area. Repeat as necessary.

SPIRAL YARN

These yarns require Z singles of different thicknesses and can also be called bead or gimp yarns. As you spin the yarns, the differences in the singles create a spiral effect.

Holding both yarns firmly, S ply the two singles together, treadling slowly. Allow the finer yarn to move straight into the orifice while holding the thicker singles at 45 degrees.

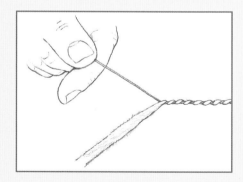

KNOT YARN

This two-ply yarn has regular knots of one or other of the singles along its length, introduced during the plying process. The yarn is also called knop and cloud yarn.

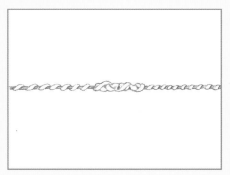

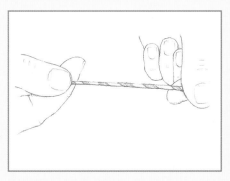

1 Spin two Z singles with a high twist (otherwise they will break). Hold the singles in separate hands and S ply. Make the knots, as the hands move forward towards the orifice, by winding one yarn round the other in a figure eight movement, at right angles to the other yarn.

2 Bring the yarns back together while the ply between the knots is forming. If the knots are made with alternate colors, you will use equal amounts of yarn from each bobbin.

MARL YARN

This spinning technique produces two colors in a singles yarn. The easiest way to produce marl yarn is with commercial tops. You can produce further marl yarns by plying one marl singles yarn with a solid-color singles yarn.

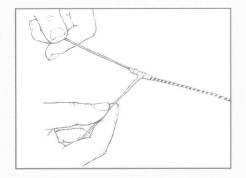

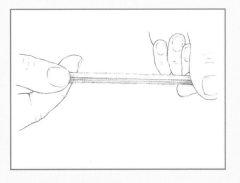

1 Peel a narrow length of tops from two lengths of tops. Draft these narrow lengths by hand to allow the fibers to slide apart easily. Holding the two colors parallel, allow even amounts of fibers from each color to enter the drafting area.

2 This method produces an even marl. Allowing more of one or other of the colors to be drafted gives an uneven marl. Ply two of these marl singles together.

TUFT YARN

The tufts in this yarn can be made from small bits of unspun fleece, small pieces of spun thread or small pieces of a different fiber. They are added during plying. This yarn is sometimes called a knickerbocker yarn.

Lay small pieces of chosen fiber or spun thread on your knee. Keeping the two Z spun singles as far apart as possible, use one hand to drop the tufts in the space just as the twist is about to run in. Work while the twist is running back towards you.

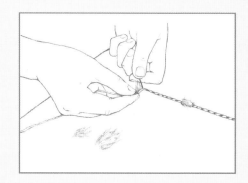

SNARL YARN

These three-ply yarns have small, highly twisted areas of doubled thread protruding from the yarn, which are introduced during plying. Yarns that are composed of three or more singles are called composite yarns. A simpler, but less stable, version of this yarn can be produced with just two singles. Taking two of the highly twisted Z spun yarns, S ply them together, allowing one to twist back on itself.

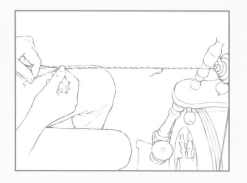

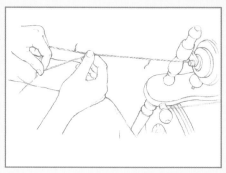

1 Spin three highly twisted Z spun yarns. Z ply two of the yarns. Keeping one of them taut, allow the other to snarl (twist back on itself) at regular intervals along the yarn.

2 S ply this yarn with the remaining Z singles, adjusting the snarls evenly as you go.

CREPE YARN

This composite yarn uses four Z singles. It is often called a cable yarn and the effect is produced by plying.

Ply two of the Z spun singles in the S direction, adding extra twist, so that when doubled back on themselves the folded end is closed. Repeat with the other two Z singles. Ply the two two-ply yarns in a Z direction to create a balanced yarn.

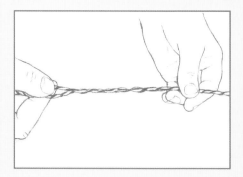

DIAMOND YARN

This composite yarn forms a diamond pattern with two fine singles over a bulky singles. The pattern is formed during the plying process.

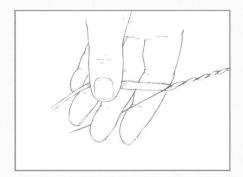

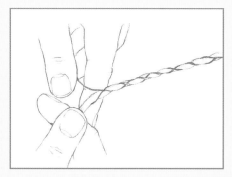

1 Spin one bulky Z singles, the central core, and two fine Z singles. Ply the central core and one of the fine singles S, putting in more twist than you normally would for a balanced ply.

2 Then ply this yarn with the other single, Z – the fine singles will form a diamond shape around the core yarn.

CORE SPUN YARN

This is a composite yarn with three components, sometimes called a bead yarn. In some cases the core and binder yarns can be commercially spun yarns. The effects occur in the plying process.

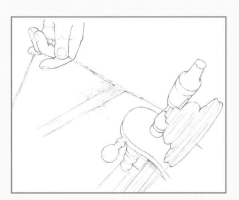

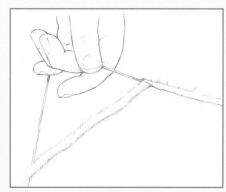

1 Spin two Z spun singles (one for the core yarn and one for the binder) with a high degree of twist. Draft separate fibers into a long roving (see Worsted spinning on page 19) and attach to one of the singles (the core).

2 Using a Z twist and holding the roving at a 45-degree angle, allow it to wrap around the singles. S ply with the remaining Z singles (the binder).

BEAD YARN

This composite yarn uses beads threaded onto one of the components during plying.

1 Spin two Z singles with a high degree of twist. Thread a commercial sewing thread with beads and Z ply this with one of the Z singles, feeding the beads in as you go.

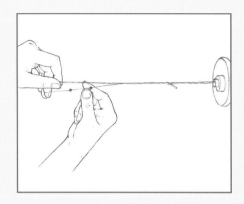

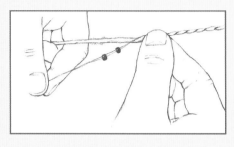

2 S ply this yarn with the remaining Z singles.

Fancy silk yarn techniques

Some of the silk spinning techniques also produce fancy yarns. The hand spinner can use the silk fiber from broken cocoons and other waste products of the commercial silk industry to create a variety of luxurious yarns.

Throwsters' waste

Throwsters' waste is a by-product of the silk-reeling industry and consists of cut lengths of reeled silk, possibly still with gum in it. It is available from suppliers in both gummed and de-gummed qualities. Irregularities are introduced into the yarn during carding (see Carding on pages 10–11).

  If you wish to spin throwsters' waste first of all de-gum the fibers if necessary. To do this place the fibers in a pan kept especially for textile work (not a pan used for food), with cold water, soap flakes and a small amount of washing soda. The amounts will depend on the pH of your water supply – hard water requires more soap and washing soda than soft water.

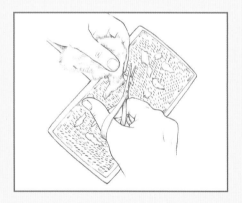

1 Cut the fibers into small pieces, the smaller the better. Place the pieces on one of a pair of carders; do not put too many on at once.

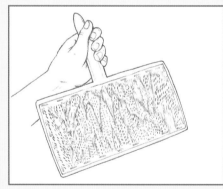

2 Begin to card gently. The reeled silk will break down into short fibers. When sufficiently carded, roll into a rolag and spin with the long draw technique (see page 18). It can be spun on its own or blended with other silk fibers or fibers from animal or vegetable sources.

MAWATA

Mawata, also known as silk 'caps' or 'hankies', are made from de-gummed cocoons. When prepared they can be spun from the hankie, or the unspun fibers can be wrapped around a core (see Core spun yarn on page 27). Irregularities are inherent in the nature of the fibers.

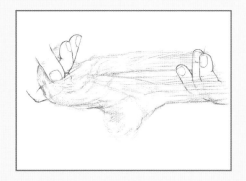

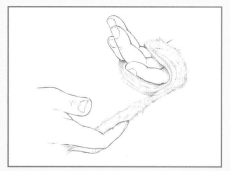

1 Hold the mawata hankie in both hands and push your fingers through. With your fingers through the mawata, firmly pull your hands apart, drawing out the fibers to a manageable thickness.

2 When the whole hankie has been pulled to a consistent thickness, wind the fibers round your hand to store them ready for spinning.

DE-GUMMED COCOONS

When silk moths emerge naturally from cocoons both long and short fibers are present. This is not desirable in the commercial silk industry as it is not easy to spin a consistent yarn from a miscellany of fiber lengths. However, hand spinners can turn this to advantage and produce beautifully textured, irregular yarns.

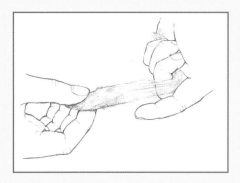

To spin the de-gummed cocoons, tease out a few fibers from the cocoon, attach to a leader on the bobbin or spindle and gently draw the silk fibers out, letting the twist run into the fibers. The natural irregularities in the fibers will add character to the yarn.

 Tip When you want to sample new fibers and you do not have an empty bobbin available, pass a loop of yarn around a partially filled bobbin and attach the new fibers to this.

shortwool
and down

The dense, woolly fleece of these enchanting sheep is a joy to spin and knits into gloriously cozy garments.

reflection

Amounts
To spin a 4 oz (100 g) hank of yarn, you will need 2½ oz (60 g) Shropshire tops in dark grey and 1½ oz (40 g) yellow wool/silk fibers in yellow.

Staple length
5–10 cm (2–4 in)

Method
1 Card the wool and silk fibers together to make an even blend (see pages 10–11).
2 Use a spindle or wheel to Z spin two singles yarns using the long draw technique (see page 18).
3 S ply the two singles yarns together (see page 20).

Golden reflections on the surface of the dark waters of a stream are recreated in this yarn that uses natural white and dark grey Shropshire fleece, the white blended with silk and dyed naturally with saffron for a fabulous yellow. The soft matt texture of the fleece and the depth of its color make a dramatic contrast with the luster of the silk. The impact of this light, airy yarn will make a statement whether used as an evening wrap or an autumn jacket.

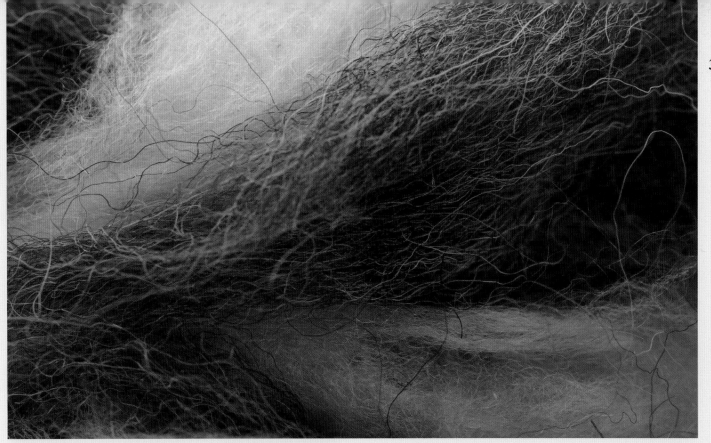

Silk glistens against wool, like the sun upon water.

chestnut

The lively little sheep that inhabit the Shetland Isles are characterized by a wonderful range of natural colors in their fleece. Our yarn is a blend of dark and light, reminiscent of the shaded chestnut shells of nature's winter bounty. Soft enough for a baby's shawl, yet strong enough to use for a tough guy's sweater, this versatile fleece is a pleasure to spin.

Amounts
To spin a 4 oz (100 g) hank of yarn, you will need 4 oz (100 g) of a commercially prepared blend of naturally colored Shetland fibers.

Staple length
5–10 cm (2–4 in)

Method
1 Use a spindle or wheel to Z spin two bobbins of medium fine singles using the long draw technique (see page 18).
2 S ply the singles together (see page 20).

Light and soft, Shetland yarn will enfold you in its warmth.

sunset

To emphasize the soft warmth of the setting sun, color combines with technique to produce a fancy yarn using Corriedale fibers. The glow of a pink sunset forms one element of the yarn, while the snarls recall the movement of the sun behind the clouds. Use this yarn judiciously — as an accent such as a textured stripe in a plain garment.

Amounts
To spin a 4 oz (100 g) hank of yarn, you will need 2 oz (50 g) prepared Corriedale fibers in pink and 2 oz (50 g) in grey.

Staple length
3–6 in (7.5–15 cm)

Method
1 Use a wheel to Z spin a medium twist pink yarn (see pages 16–17).
2 Z spin a high twist yarn using the pink and grey fibers alternately.
3 Z ply these yarns together, allowing the pink/grey yarn to twist back on itself, creating little snarls (see page 26).
4 Z spin a fine grey yarn.
5 S ply the 2-ply yarn and the fine grey yarn together, (see page 20).

Capture the movement of color across a sunset sky.

crocus

Spinners familiar with this wonderful breed, the Falkland, also know it as the Green Sheep as sheep reared in the Falkland Islands are farmed without the use of insecticides and growth hormones. This yarn is suited to soft warm garments that will cheer the short dark days of winter, reminding us that spring will come again soon.

Amounts
To spin a 4 oz (100 g) hank of yarn, you will need 4 oz (100 g) prepared Falkland fibers randomly dyed green and pink.

Staple length
4 in (10 cm)

Method
1 Use a spindle or wheel to Z spin a bobbin of fine yarn (see pages 13–14 or 16–17).
2 Navajo ply the yarn in the S direction, keeping the colors distinct (see page 22).

These subtle greens and pinks are the colors of spring crocuses.

medium
and fine wool

Many breeds of sheep produce a medium-length fleece of a medium quality, ideal for beginners. The finest fleece comes from the Merino.

riverside

Dappled sunlight filtering through trees, casting green and grey shadows; glimpses of blue sky through branches, reflected in the water; shades of pink on the river banks – all create a summery feel. Merino wool, one of the finest wool fibers, produces a beautifully soft, lofty yarn. It can be spun fine to knit into cobweb shawls and lightweight knitwear, or thicker for warm hats, scarves and mittens. It takes dye well and is available in a huge range of colored tops.

Amounts

To spin a 4 oz (100 g) hank of 2-ply yarn, you will need 1 oz (25 g) Merino tops in air force blue, 1 oz (25 g) in silver grey, 1¼ oz (35 g) in lime green and ½ oz (15 g) in deep pink.

Staple length

3 in (7.5 cm)

Method

1 Split each color, lengthways, into an equal number of sections.
2 Using a spindle or wheel, Z spin one section of air force blue and one section of silver grey side by side, drawing out the fibers equally (see page 25). Continue until all sections are used.
3 Repeat with light lime and deep pink.
4 S ply, producing a marl yarn (see page 25).

Soft and lofty, this yarn
is inspired by dappled
sunlight.

woodland

The Jacob fleece gives a wonderful selection of natural creams, greys and very dark browns. The dark shades are almost black on lambs, but lighten as the sheep ages. There is quite a difference between fleeces, ranging from almost all brown to nearly all white with light spotting. This means that when you make up a sweater or a hat in Jacob, you can rely on a variety of shades to give you interesting natural colors and accidental patterns without the need for dyeing.

Amounts
To spin a 4 oz (100 g) hank of 2-ply yarn, you will need 2 oz (50 g) Jacob fleece in brown and 2 oz (50 g) in natural white.

Staple length
3¼–6 in (8–15 cm)

Method
1 Lightly blend the brown and white fleece together with carders so that the two colors remain evident (see pages 10–11).
2 Use a spindle or wheel to Z spin two singles of a chunky thickness (see pages 13–14 or 16–17).
3 S ply the two singles together (see page 20).

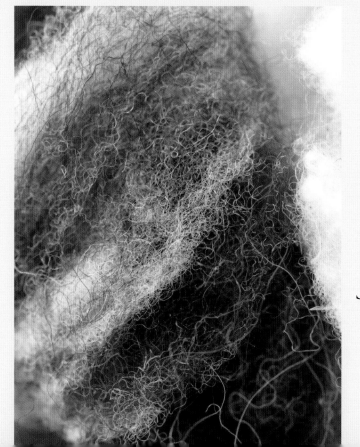

Warm yet light in weight, Jacob is the perfect wool to spin for a cozy sweater.

lake

Rippling water in greys and blues, with white and lilac reflections, inspires a lovely light slub yarn spun from a medium fleece. The good quality, all-purpose wool fibers chosen are ideal for beginners and are suitable for cosy sweaters, hats, scarves and gloves. English 56's is an expression of the diameter of the fibers in the Bradford Count – the higher the count, the finer the fibers – and is a blend of several fleeces of the same count.

Amounts

To spin a 4 oz (100 g) hank of 2-ply slub yarn, you will need 2 ¾ oz (75 g) English 56's tops in white, ½ oz (10 g) in deep blue, ½ oz (10 g) in lilac and ¼ oz (5 g) in sand.

Staple length

4 in (10 cm)

Method

1 Lightly blend ¼ oz (5 g) deep blue, ¼ oz (5 g) lilac and ⅛ oz (2.5 g) sand with 1 oz (25 g) white with carders so that the colors remain evident.
2 Use a spindle or wheel to Z spin a fine singles (see pages 13–14 or 16–17).
3 Lightly blend the remaining dyed tops with the remaining white tops and Z spin a medium, regularly slubbed, yarn (see page 24).
4 S ply together to give a balanced yarn (see page 20).

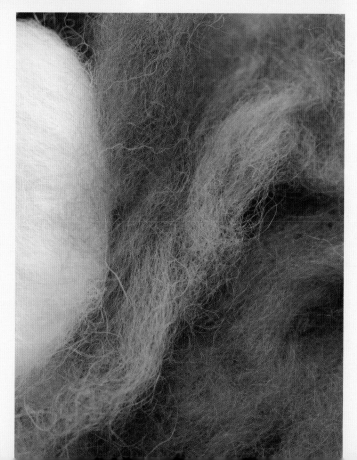

Allow this light slub yarn to ripple around you as a soft scarf.

raindrops

Greens and lemons with clear, crystal droplets of rain, created here by adding tiny beads, give a fresh, spring feel. Texel sheep, originally from the island of Texel off the Dutch coast, are now quite common throughout the world. The fleece they produce is of a medium quality and staple length, making it a useful general-purpose fleece, ideal for the beginner.

Amounts
To spin a 4 oz (100 g) hank of 2-ply bead yarn, you will need 1¼ oz (33 g) Texel tops in green, 1¼ oz (33 g) in lime and 1¼ oz (33 g) in yellow. You will also need 1 bobbin of fine sewing cotton in green and 200 very small clear seed beads.

Staple length
3 in (7.5 cm)

Method
1 Lightly blend the green, lime and yellow fleece together with carders so that the three colours remain evident

2 Use a wheel to spin two-thirds of the wool into a medium Z spun yarn (see pages 16–17).

3 Spin the remaining wool into a fine Z spun yarn.

4 Thread the beads onto the green sewing thread and Z ply with the fine Z spun yarn, spacing the beads at regular intervals (see page 28).

5 S ply this yarn with the medium Z spun yarn (see page 20).

Feel spring-like with greens, lemons and crystal drops.

longwool
and luster

These versatile fleeces are exactly as described, long and lustrous. The hand spinner can achieve both a luster worsted and a fine woollen yarn from the fibers.

cloud

Wensleydale sheep are a favorite with many hand spinners, the engaging animals looking as though they have fashioned their wool into dreadlocks! Available in natural colors as well as a white that dyes beautifully, this fleece will reward the spinner with wonderful soft, warm yarns for winter wraps.

Amounts
To spin a 4 oz (100 g) hank of yarn, you will need 3 oz (75 g) prepared Wensleydale fibers in white and 1 oz (25 g) in pale blue.

Staple length
12 in (30 cm)

Method
1 Use a spindle or wheel to Z spin a slub yarn with the white fleece, making the slubs longer than normal (see page 24).
2 Z spin a fine worsted yarn with the pale blue yarn (see page 19).
3 S ply the slub yarn and the fine worsted yarn together (see page 20).

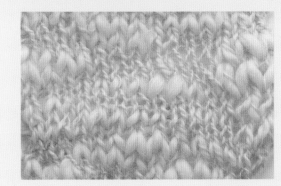

Light as air and fluffy clouds, Wensleydale wool will wrap you in coziness.

driftwood

Bluefaced Leicester is classified as a longwool and luster breed, but it has a shorter staple length than most of its grouping and is easier for less experienced spinners to use. Suitable for warm woolly cardigans, hats, socks and gloves, this versatile fleece has endless possibilities for you to explore your creativity. Available in a range of natural colors and white, this yarn is spun in a blend of undyed fibers, with the addition of tussah silk to add extra zing!

Amounts
To spin a 4 oz (100 g) hank of yarn, you will need 4 oz (100 g) Bluefaced Leicester blended tops and ½ oz (10 g) tussah silk.

Staple length
4–6 in (10–15 cm)

Method
1 Use a spindle or wheel to Z spin two bobbins of the blended tops (see pages 13–14 or 16–17).
2 S ply the yarns together, adding tiny pieces of tussah silk as you spin (see page 26).

The natural shades of this wool are subtle as the color of driftwood.

sunbeam

Not as soft as Wensleydale or Bluefaced Leicester wool, Lincoln wool is best used for items such as bags and soft furnishings. A very hardwearing luster yarn; use it to make items that will take a lot of punishment and it will reward you with a long life. The fleece takes dye well, as in this yarn that recalls a grey sky split with sunbeams.

Amounts
To spin a 4 oz (100 g) hank of yarn, you will need 2 oz (50 g) Lincoln fibers in grey and 2 oz (50 g)) in yellow.

Staple length
8–15 in (20–37.5 cm)

Method
1 Use a wheel to Z spin the grey fibers into a medium yarn (see pages 16–17).
2 Z spin the yellow fibers into a finer yarn.
3 S ply the yarns together, allowing the yellow yarn to make a repeated figure eight knot around the grey yarn at intervals (see page 25).

Bright and strong, use this hardwearing yarn to make an impact!

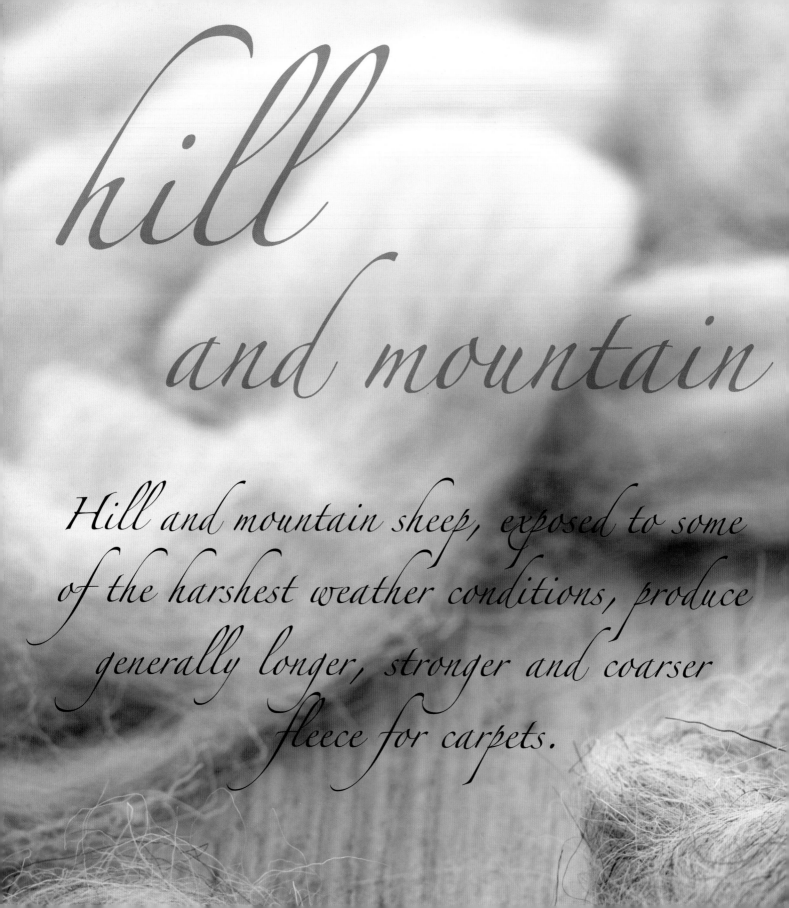

hill
and mountain

Hill and mountain sheep, exposed to some of the harshest weather conditions, produce generally longer, stronger and coarser fleece for carpets.

pebble

The Black Welsh Mountain sheep produces the blackest of all the fleeces and is finer than the white fleece of the Welsh Mountain. This Black Welsh Mountain wool, blended with silk, is surprisingly soft and is available ready blended and in tops form. This yarn lends itself to stylish knitted or crocheted garments.

Amounts
To spin a 4 oz (100 g) hank of 2-ply yarn, you will need 4 oz (100 g) Black Welsh Mountain and silk blend tops.

Staple length
3 in (7.5 cm)

Method
1   Use a spindle or wheel to Z spin two bobbins of singles (see pages 13–14 or 16–17).
2   S ply the singles together (see page 20).

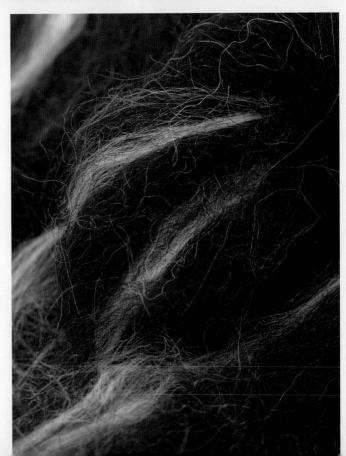

Encase yourself in a surprisingly soft black and cream yarn.

shell

Shells tossed in crashing waves and bleached by the sun inspire a yarn created from a dense Swaledale fleece spun in a spiral, swirling round a finer singles. Spun in this way, these long, coarse fibers are ideal to add a touch of texture to hand-woven or knitted rugs. The hardy Swaledale sheep is from the region of the same name, high up in the Pennines of North Yorkshire, England.

Amounts

To spin a 4 oz (100 g) hank of 2-ply spiral yarn, you will need 4 oz (100 g) Swaledale tops.

Staple length

6 in (15 cm)

Method

1 Take 3 oz (75 g) of the tops and Z spin, using a spindle or wheel, into a thick singles (see pages 13–14 or 16–17).

2 With the remaining 1 oz (25 g), Z spin a fine singles.

3 S ply the two singles together, holding the thicker yarn at a 45-degree angle to the fine yarn, allowing it to spiral around the fine yarn (see page 24).

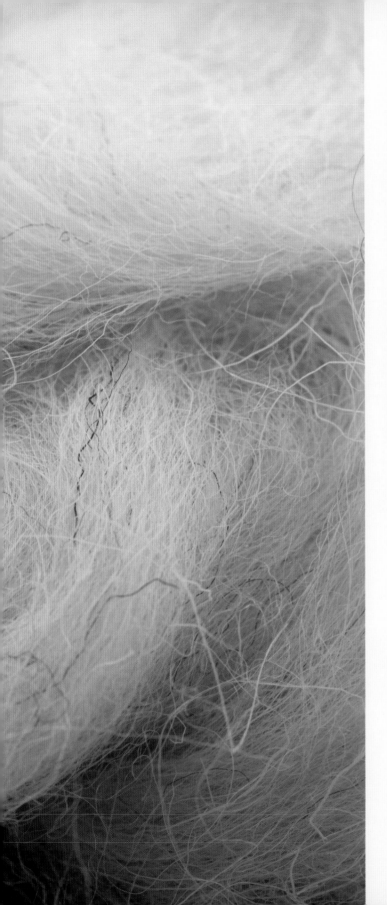

Wave-tossed shells,
bleached by the sun
inspired this yarn.

slate

Herdwick sheep, from the Lake District, England, are thought to have Scandinavian origins. The lambs are born black and the fleece grows progressively lighter as the sheep gets older. Spun into a slub yarn, dark grey and light grey Herdwick tops reflect the colors of slate. This yarn will give lovely texture to a hardwearing hand-woven or knitted bag.

Amounts
To spin a 4 oz (100 g) hank of 2-ply slub yarn, you will need 3 oz (75 g) Herdwick tops in dark grey and 1 oz (25 g) in light grey.

Staple length
6 in (15 cm)

Method
1 Using dark grey tops, peel off ½ in (12.5 mm) wide sections.
2 Use a spindle or wheel to Z spin a slub yarn (see page 24).
3 Z spin the light grey tops into a fine singles (see pages 13–14 or 16–17).
4 S ply the slub yarn and the fine singles together (see page 20).

Dark and light grey Herdwick tops reflect the colors of slate.

rare wool

The fleece from rare sheep is a joy,
full of the character and eccentricity
that has been bred out of
its conformist cousins.

popcorn

The Cotswold lion, as these animals are affectionately known, are the sheep on which the medieval English wool trade was based – the Lord Chancellor still sits on the 'woolsack' in recognition of the past importance of wool. One Cotswold sheep can produce a fleece weighing up to 37 lb (17 kg), and the breed has improved bloodlines of sheep all over the world. This yarn will keep you warm in the icy blasts of winter, and will take a fraction of such a huge fleece.

Amounts
To spin a 4 oz (100 g) hank of yarn, you will need 4 oz (100 g) combed Cotswold fibers.

Staple length
8–10 in (20–25 cm)

Method
1   Use a wheel to Z spin a fine singles – this will be the core yarn (see pages 16–17).
2   Wrap the core yarn in a Z direction, with fleece (see page 27)
3   Z spin a fine singles – this will be the binder yarn (see pages 16–17).
4   S ply the wrapped core and binder together (see page 20).

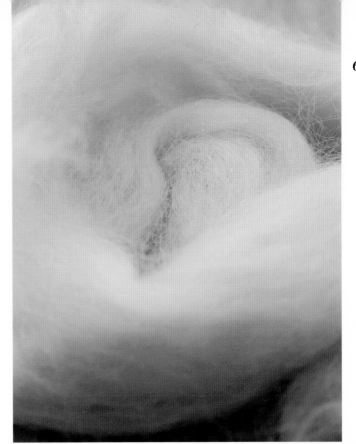

The Cotswold sheep has changed very little in the last five hundred years.

sunrise

Whiteface Dartmoor are a very old breed of sheep and are noted for their ability to survive the harsh winters on the moors. The fibers have a strong crimp, making the wool easy to spin, but the adult fleece is coarse and used chiefly for carpeting. The lambswool clip is valuable and this striking yarn is spun from a shearling fleece that is considerably softer than the adult equivalent. Use it for an outdoor sweater or rug.

Amounts

To spin a 4 oz (100 g) hank of yarn, you will need 2 oz (50 g) Whiteface Dartmoor lambswool fibers in black, 1 oz (25 g) in orange and 1 oz (25 g) in yellow.

Staple length

6–8 in (15–20 cm)

Method

1 Use a wheel to Z spin the black fibers into a thick singles (see pages 16–17).

2 Z spin the orange and the yellow fibers into two fine singles yarns.

3 S ply all three yarns together (see page 27). The fine singles should wrap around the core to form a diamond shape.

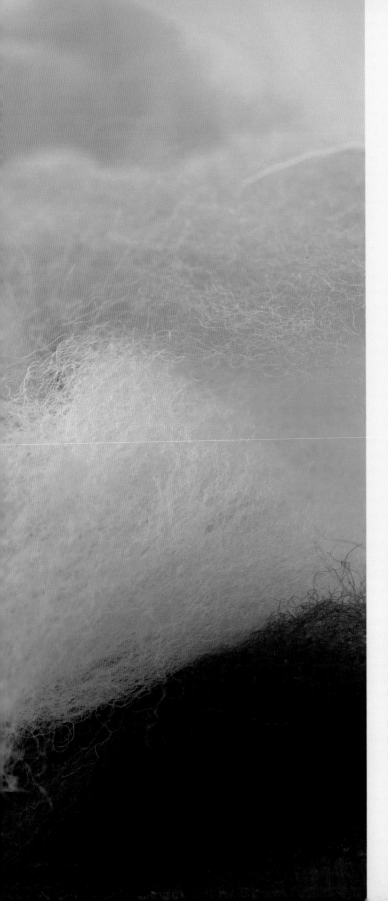

The Whiteface Dartmoor endures hot summers and dark winters.

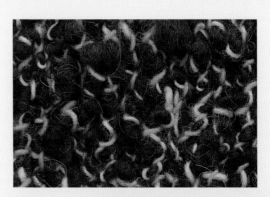

coconut

The Manx Loughton breed of little brown sheep, descendants of the primitive sheep native to the north of Scotland and the Scottish islands, has become established on the Isle of Man. The colored wool is a good choice for a naturally colored sweater or cardigan. This yarn combines the natural color of the Manx sheep with the white silk of mawata, creating an impression of the fibrous coconut fruit and shell.

Amounts
To spin a 4 oz (100 g) hank of yarn, you will need 3 oz (75 g) Manx Loughton fibers and 1 oz (25 g) prepared mawata.

Staple length
3–4 in (7.5–10 cm)

Method
1 Use a wheel to Z spin a fine yarn with the Manx Loughton – this will be the core yarn (see pages 16–17).
2 Wrap this core yarn in a Z direction with the mawata (see page 27).
3 Z spin a second fine yarn with the Manx Loughton – this will be the binder yarn (see pages 16–17).
4 S ply the core spun and binder yarns (see page 20).

Tender silk wrapped in Manx wool echoes white coconut flesh in its shell.

mist

A charming characteristic of the Portland sheep is that the lambs are born a foxy red color. This changes to white or grey during their first few months, though occasionally a red hair is found in the adult fleece. Classified as shortwool and down, the fibers are ideal for hand-knitting yarns. Our Mist yarn is light and warm – use it for the luxurious warmth of a cosy throw or blanket.

Amounts
To spin a 4 oz (100 g) hank of yarn, you will need 3 oz (75 g) carded Portland fibers in white and 1 oz (25 g) in grey.

Staple length
3–4 in (7.5–10 cm)

Method
1 Use a wheel to spin a fine yarn with half the grey fibers – this will be the core yarn (see pages 16–17).
2 Wrap the core yarn with the white fibers in a Z direction (see page 27).
3 Z spin a fine yarn with the remaining grey fibers – this will be the binder yarn (see pages 16–17).
4 S ply the wrapped core and binder together (see page 20).

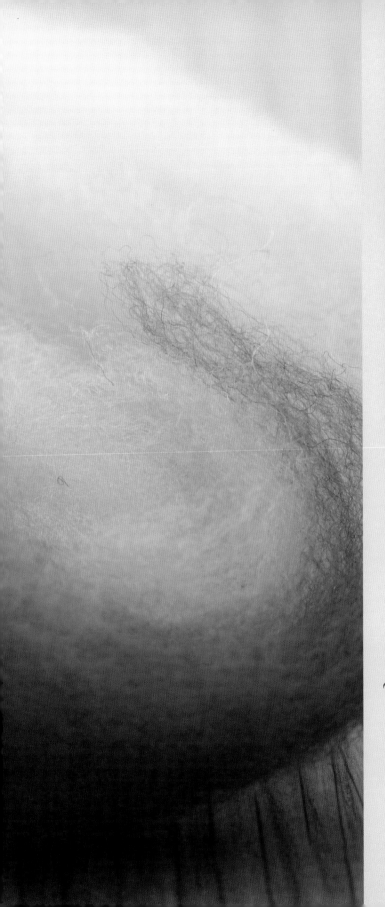

A soft, light yarn to float around you in the chill of an early morning.

animal hair

These fibers, smoother than wool, require more twist when spinning into yarn. Fibers range in fineness from Angora goat to cashmere.

lavender

Soft pinks, lilacs and mossy greens contrast with navy blue, capturing the subtle colors of lavender. This yarn is created from ready-dyed kid mohair and is simply Z spun and S plied. Mohair fibers can be as long as 12 in (30 cm) if shorn once a year, so it is general to shear the animals twice yearly. The fibers are usually spun into a worsted yarn and are useful for loop or bouclé yarns.

Amounts
To spin a 4 oz (100 g) hank of yarn, you will need 4 oz (100 g) of ready-dyed kid mohair fibers.

Staple length
6 in (15 cm)

Method
1 Comb the kid mohair (see page 12).
2 Use a spindle or a wheel to Z spin two fine singles with a little extra twist (see pages 13–14 or 16–17).
3 S ply the two fine singles together (see page 20).

Soft pinks, lilacs and mossy greens capture the color of lavender.

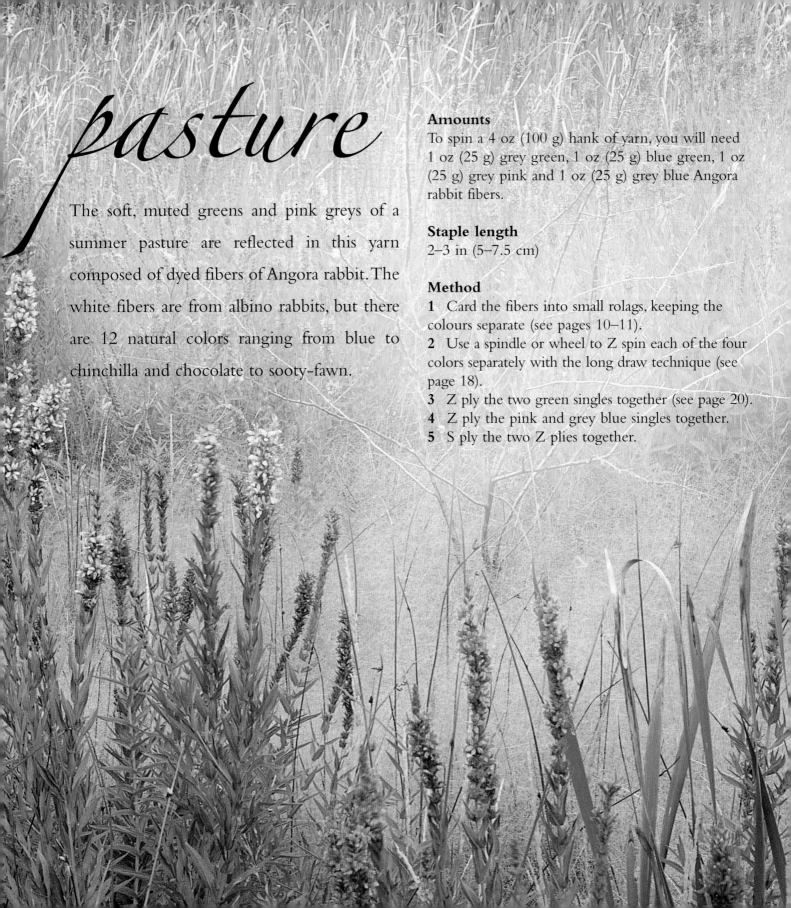

pasture

The soft, muted greens and pink greys of a summer pasture are reflected in this yarn composed of dyed fibers of Angora rabbit. The white fibers are from albino rabbits, but there are 12 natural colors ranging from blue to chinchilla and chocolate to sooty-fawn.

Amounts

To spin a 4 oz (100 g) hank of yarn, you will need 1 oz (25 g) grey green, 1 oz (25 g) blue green, 1 oz (25 g) grey pink and 1 oz (25 g) grey blue Angora rabbit fibers.

Staple length

2–3 in (5–7.5 cm)

Method

1 Card the fibers into small rolags, keeping the colours separate (see pages 10–11).

2 Use a spindle or wheel to Z spin each of the four colors separately with the long draw technique (see page 18).

3 Z ply the two green singles together (see page 20).

4 Z ply the pink and grey blue singles together.

5 S ply the two Z plies together.

The natural colors of the Angora rabbit range from blue to chocolate.

autumn leaves

These possum fibers were over dyed, randomly, with terracotta, ochre and moss green acid dyes to recreate autumn colors. Possum is considered a pest in Australia and New Zealand, but its short fibers, comprising down and guard hair, are now acknowledged as a valuable 'eco' fiber and are blended with Merino on a commercial scale. Products from possum-wool blend yarns are surprisingly resilient despite their light weight.

Amounts
To spin a 4 oz (100 g) hank of yarn, you will need 4 oz (100 g) randomly dyed possum fur.

Staple length
1 in (2–3 cm)

Method
1 Card the dyed possum fur into small rolags (see pages 10–11).
2 Use a spindle or wheel to Z spin two bobbins with the long draw technique (see page 18).
3 S ply the yarns together (see page 20).

Autumn leaves contain
myriad colors.

silk

The industrious silkworm creates
a variety of fibers for the hand spinner
that can be used to create exciting
and original yarns.

blossom

Warm as cashmere and one of the lightest natural fibers in the world, this silk fiber spins into a textured, yet lustrous, yarn. It knits up into a gorgeous lightweight fabric, suitable for elegant shawls and chic sweaters. Choose subtle pastels, such as this gentle pink, to blend with the natural shades of undyed tussah silk.

Amounts

To spin a 4 oz (100 g) hank of 2-ply silk yarn, you will need 2 oz (50 g) tussah silk tops in ecru and 2 oz (50 g) throwsters' waste in pink.

Method

1 Use a spindle or wheel to Z spin the silk tops with the worsted technique into a fine singles (see page 19).

2 Card the throwsters' waste into rolags (see pages 10–11 and 28).

3 Z spin the throwsters' waste rolags using the long draw technique (see page 18).

4 S ply the tussah yarn and throwsters' waste yarn together (see page 20).

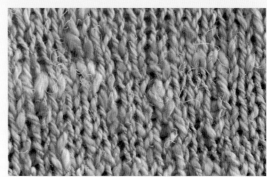

As soft as spring:
warm rose pink and
natural cream.

down

This combination of natural silk fibers creates a yarn that is as fine and delicate as the fluffy seedheads that inspired it. Knitted on a generously sized set of needles, the resulting fabric will feel as light as air on your shoulders, and is perfect for a precious evening stole or wrap.

Amounts
To spin a 4 oz (100 g) hank of 2-ply yarn, you will need 2 oz (50 g) tussah silk tops, 2 oz (50 g) cultivated silk tops and approximately 1 oz (20 g) tussah noils.

Staple length
Noils – 1 in (2.5 cm)

Method
1 Use a spindle or wheel to S spin the two silk tops separately, using the worsted method (see page 19). Keep the yarn as fine and even as possible.
2 Z ply the yarns together, catching a tiny amount of tussah noils between the plies every 2–4 in (5–10 cm), making sure that it is well anchored (see page 26).

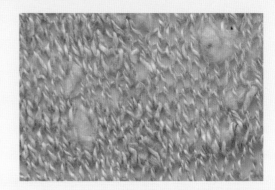

This thistledown yarn
will make a luxurious
and floaty fabric.

kingfisher

Inspired by the fleeting glimpse of a kingfisher in glorious plumage, this yarn relies for its dramatic appeal on the vivid blue, turquoise and orange-tan borrowed from this glamorous little bird. Light as a feather and with the same insulating properties, this yarn will knit into a beautiful fabric. The worsted technique emphasizes the luster of the silk.

Amounts

To spin a 4 oz (100 g) hank of 3-ply yarn, you will need 4 oz (100 g) of multicolored silk tops.

Method

1 Use a spindle or wheel to Z spin the tops, in manageable lengths, using the worsted method to emphasize the luster of the silk (see page 19).

2 When you have a full bobbin, use the Navajo method to create a 3-ply yarn (see page 22).

Jewel-like colors from Nature's paintbox.

vegetable fibers

Vegetable fibers come from two sources: leaves, which produce coarser fibers for twine and string, or stems, sometimes called bast fibers.

lapis lazuli

Cotton grows in very warm or hot climates and usually comes as an off white color, as in these fibers, but it is now also grown in a natural brown or green color. Soya fibers are a by-product of the tofu manufacturing process; they are soft and lustrous and resemble tussah silk. This fancy yarn is ideal for areas of detail in knitwear or weave.

Amounts
To spin a 4 oz (100 g) hank of 2-ply yarn, you will need 1 oz (25 g) textured cream carded cotton fibers, 1 oz (25 g) textured cream carded cotton fibres dyed in a dark grey blue and 2 oz (50 g) soya staple fibers.

Staple length
Textured cream carded cotton – up to ¾ in (2 cm)
Soya staple fibres – 2 in (5 cm)

Method
1 Card equal amounts of cream carded cotton with the dyed carded cotton fibers (see pages 10–11).
2 Use a spindle or wheel to Z spin the carded cotton fibers with the long draw technique (see page 18).
3 Card the soya staple fibers.
4 Z spin the carded soya fibers with the long draw technique.
5 S ply the cotton and soya singles together (see page 20).

The colored flecks recall the richness of a precious mineral.

apple

Mahogany-colored apple pips in a creamy white flesh, encased in deep red skin, suggested a spiral, beaded yarn. The lustrous ramie fibers used here are suitable for both soft thick yarn and smooth thin yarn. Ramie, a bast fiber, has been grown for centuries in China and the Far East. It is resistant to rot and mildew and is very absorbent, but is quick drying. Ramie fibers are available to hand spinners as combed tops.

Amounts
To spin a 4 oz (100 g) hank of bead yarn, you will need 3 oz (80 g) ramie tops in white and ½ oz (10 g) ramie tops dyed red. You will also need 1 bobbin of fine sewing cotton in brown and 200 dark red seed beads.

Staple length
4–10 in (10–25 cm)

Method
1   Peel off pencil-size slivers of the white ramie.
2   Use a spindle or wheel to Z spin the white ramie into a medium thick yarn with the worsted technique (see page 19).
3   Z spin the red ramie into a fine yarn (see pages 16–17).
4   Thread the beads onto the brown sewing thread and Z ply with the fine Z spun red yarn, spacing the beads, in pairs, at regular intervals (see page 28).
5   S ply the bead yarn with the medium Z spun yarn (see page 20).

Dark red seed beads shine like the glossy brown pips inside an apple.

seedling

Cool green shoots pushing through brown soil are the inspiration for this snarl yarn. Bamboo has unique anti-bacterial properties, is 100 percent biodegradable and is praised as 'the natural, green and eco-friendly new-type textile material of the 21st century'. It is noted for its breathability and coolness, so is ideal for fine knitwear, woven garments, table linens and towels.

Amounts
To spin a 4 oz (100 g) hank of 2-ply snarl yarn, you will need 2½ oz (60 g) bamboo fibres dyed green and 1½ oz (40 g) bamboo fibres dyed brown.

Staple length
1½–3 in (4–7.5 cm)

Method
1 Using a wheel, Z spin the green fibres and brown fibres on separate bobbins (see pages 16–17).
2 S ply the two singles together, allowing the green singles to snarl in groups of three (see page 26).

New shoots have a lovely luster, which is reflected in the use of the bamboo.

fancy fibers

Most fancy fibers are products of the recycling process, such as recycled plastic bottles, denim jean fibers and sari silk, or are left after carding like linen noils.

rainbow

The colors of a rainbow are the inspiration for this yarn, spun from rainbow-dyed, de-gummed silk cocoons. This yarn is spun using the colors in succeeding order: red, orange, yellow, green and blue, but you may wish to vary the order of colors.

Amounts

To make a 4 oz (100 g) hank of yarn, you will need 4 oz (100 g) of rainbow-dyed de-gummed silk cocoons.

Method

1 Use a spindle or wheel to Z spin a fairly fine yarn, working directly from the cocoon and pulling the fiber out as you spin (see page 29). Do not worry about the occasional slub that will occur naturally.

2 When you have a full bobbin, Navajo ply the yarn to give you a three-strand yarn, keeping the colors distinct if you wish (see page 22).

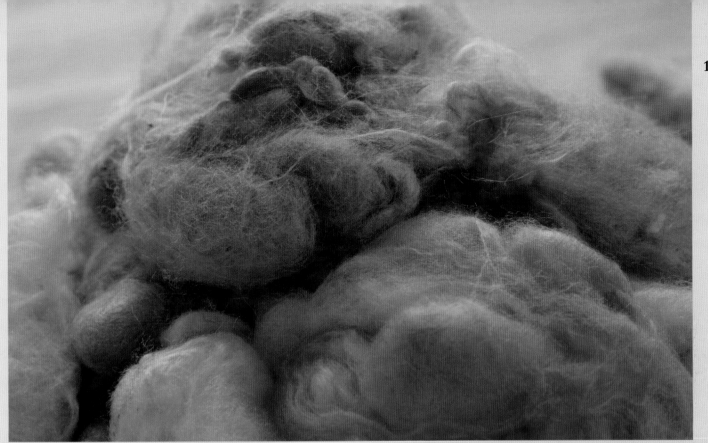

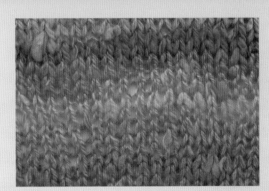

Spin a rainbow of silk with dyed de-gummed silk cocoons.

creeper

When dyed pink and mixed with a grey wool, the linen noils in this yarn resemble the stems of a rampant Virginia creeper. Bamboo has a natural whiteness that means it does not need to be bleached. Its fibers are soft and lustrous, take dye readily and are ideal for the tufts in this yarn. This unusual mixed yarn would provide lovely texture to a warm, chunky knitted garment.

Amounts
To spin a 4 oz (100 g) hank of 2-ply tuft yarn, you will need 1½ oz (40 g) linen noils dyed a dark pink, 2 oz (50 g) natural grey wool and ½ oz (10 g) randomly dyed bamboo fibers.

Staple length
Linen noils – up to ¾ in (2 cm)
Bamboo – 1½–3 in (4–7.5 cm)
Natural grey wool – 4 in (10 cm)

Method
1 Card together the natural grey wool and the pink linen noils (see pages 10–11).
2 Use a wheel to Z spin onto two bobbins using the long draw technique (see page 18).
3 S ply the two singles and insert small tufts of the random dyed bamboo fibers (see page 26).

Exciting and unusual mixes can be made from your stash of leftover fibers.

frost

The irregular texture of crisp frost and snow makes an ideal subject for a yarn that uses recycled plastic bottle fibers. The recycling process involves melting the bottles to produce a thick liquid that is extruded through showerhead-like devices to create fibrous, polyester strands. These strands are stretched, crimped and cut into short pieces before being manufactured into fleece fabric.

Amounts
To spin a 4 oz (100 g) hank of 2-ply yarn, you will need 2½ oz (60 g) tri-lobal nylon fibres in bright white and 1½ oz (40 g) recycled plastic bottle fibers.

Staple length
Tri-lobal nylon fibres – 3–5 in (7.5–12 cm)
Recycled plastic bottle fibres – 1–1½ in (2.5–4 cm)

Method
1 Use a spindle or a wheel. Take manageable handfuls of the recycled plastic bottle fibers and Z spin as it comes from the hand (see pages 13–14 or 16–17). Do not try to straighten the fibers, so as to keep the frosty effect. Z spin one bobbin of Z singles.
2 On a second bobbin Z spin the tri-lobal nylon.
3 S ply the two bobbins of yarn together (see page 20).

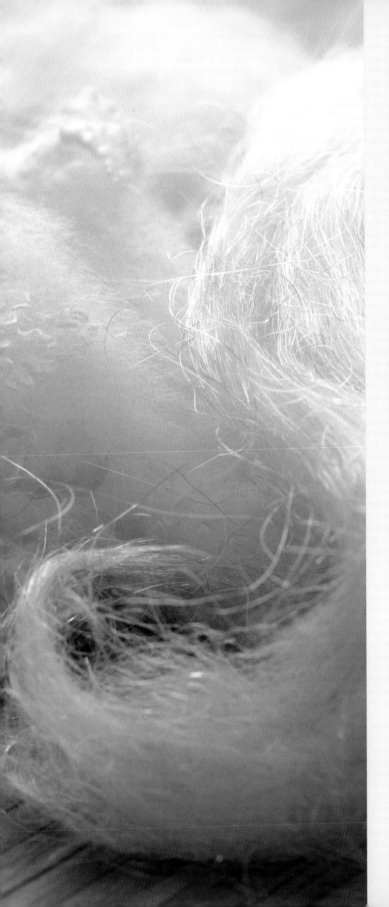

The sparkle in this yarn is obtained from tri-lobal nylon fibers.

Glossary

Bast fibers Long fibers produced from the stems of plants.

Bouclé Another name for a loop yarn, characterized by circular projections from a core.

Carding The preparation of fibers for woollen spinning using the long draw technique.

Carders The tools used for carding. They consist of two flat pieces of wood with handles and are covered with a 'cloth' pierced by short bent wires that 'brush' the fibers.

Clip The technical term for a shorn wool fleece.

Combing A method of preparation for worsted spinning so that the fibers are separated and even.

Composite yarns Yarns composed of more than one type of singles and/or more than one type of ply.

Core A fine yarn that forms the basis for a composite yarn.

Double drive One long band that controls both flyer and bobbin on a spinning wheel.

Drafting To pull fibers from the mass in a thickness that is easy to spin.

Felt Wool arranged in layers and compacted into sheets with the aid of soap, water, heat and friction. Felting will also occur if woollen yarn, fibers or garments are mistreated during washing or drying.

Fleece The shorn coat of a sheep.

Flyer A U-shaped device that enables the twist to be put into the yarn at the same time it winds onto the bobbin of a spinning wheel.

Half-hitch A simple knot used to attach the leader to the top of the spindle.

Irregularities Natural or deliberate variations in preparation, spinning and plying of yarns.

Lazy Kate A storage unit for spare bobbins, used when plying.

Leader A short length of yarn, commercial or hand spun, used to attach fibers to the spindle or bobbin at the start of the spinning process.

Lock A single section of fleece.

Mawata A Japanese name for stretched de-gummed, pierced cocoons layered one on top of the other and used as wadding for garments. 'Hankies' are made by stretching the de-gummed cocoons over nails on a square frame. 'Caps' are made by stretching them over upturned basins.

Navajo ply A method of making three-ply yarn from one bobbin.

Niddy noddy A device for winding yarn into skeins.

Noils Short fibers removed during the combing process.

Orifice The hole at the front of the spinning wheel through which the yarn is twisted.

Pass The passage of one carder across the surface of another to straighten the fibers.

Ply To spin two or more yarns together to balance the twist – two-ply yarn is made from two singles yarns, three-ply yarn is made from three singles yarns. These hand spun yarns may or may not correspond to similar designations in use for industrially spun yarns.

Rolag A roll of carded fibers used for spinning with long draw technique.

Roving Commercially combed or carded fibers that are drawn out to a thin ribbon, then slightly twisted.

Singles The unit of spun yarn on one bobbin or a spindle that will usually require plying before use.

Shearling The first clip from a sheep.

Skein Another word for hank.

Slub Thicker areas of undrafted fibers within a yarn.

Snarl An area of the yarn with excess twist that has doubled back on itself, either by design, as in a snarl yarn, or by accident.

Scotch tension A device to adjust the speed of the bobbin on a spinning wheel.

Staple length The length of fibers. Knowing this helps to determine which method of preparation and spinning technique to use.

S twist An anticlockwise spun yarn.

Spindle A simple hand tool for spinning fibers.

Tops Commercially prepared fibers available to spinners.

Twist The revolutions of a spindle or wheel that roll the fibers as they are drafted, causing them to unite. Bulky yarns need less twist, fine yarns need more twist.

Woollen yarn Yarn spun using the long draw technique. The yarn is prepared by carding and spun from a rolag, allowing the twist to enter the fiber supply as drafting occurs.

Whorl The weighted part of a spindle.

Worsted yarn Yarn spun using the worsted spinning technique, prepared by combing to remove short fibers and to create a parallel arrangement of fibers.

Z twist A clockwise spun yarn.

index

Acknowledgements

Authors' acknowledgements
We would like to thank Ruth Gough, of Wingham Wool Work, for
her help in supplying most the fibers for this book. Nobody gains
the experience we have, without the the inspiration and enthusiasm
of other spinners, of whom there are many. Particularly influential in
our creative development have been Linda Griffiths, Sue Hiley, Ann
Norman and Andrea Noble. Anybody who teaches, as we do, gets
more back from their students than they give, for which we are
grateful. Finally, this book would not have been written without the
love and support of our families.

Picture acknowledgements
All photography © Octopus Publishing Group Limited/
Vanessa Davies.

Except for the following:

Alamy 32; /blickwinkel 90; /Ken Kerr 88; /Art Kowalsky 78.
Ashford Handicrafts Limited 6.
Leigh Jones 36, 38, 46, 48, 56, 80, 86.
Octopus Publishing Group Limited/Jerry Harpur 104.

Publisher's acknowledgements
Thank you to Nancy Lee Child at the The Handweavers Studio for
generously lending us both spun and unspun fibers for photography.

The Handweavers Studio
29 Haroldstone Road, London, E17 7AN
Tel: 020 8521 2281
Website: www.geocities.com/athens/agora/9814/

Executive Editor **Jessica Cowie**
Managing Editor **Clare Churly**
Executive Art Editor **Leigh Jones**
Designer **Jo Tapper**
Photographer **Vanessa Davies**
Illustrator **Sheilagh Noble**
Production Manager **Simone Nauerth**